Reader's Digest **READING**

SKILL BUILDER

SILVER EDITION EDITORS

Miriam Weiss Meyer and Peter Travers, Project Editors

Barbara Antonopulos and Jacqueline Kinghorn, Editors

SILVER EDITION CONSULTANTS

Fred Chavez, Director of Programs
Los Angeles City Reading Support Services Center
Los Angeles, California

Marguerite E. Fuller, Assistant Supervisor of Language Arts
Norwalk Public Schools
Norwalk, Connecticut

Sister Maria Loyola, I.H.M., Chairperson, Reading Curriculum Committee
Archdiocese of Philadelphia
Philadelphia, Pennsylvania

Dr. John. F. Savage, Coordinator, Reading Specialist Program
Boston College, School of Education
Chestnut Hill, Massachusetts

Richard B. Solymos, Reading Resource Teacher
School Board of Broward County
Fort Lauderdale, Florida

READER'S DIGEST EDUCATIONAL DIVISION
© 1977 by Reader's Digest Services, Inc., Pleasantville, N.Y. 10570. All rights reserved, including the right to reproduce this book or parts thereof in any form.
Printed in the United States of America.
Reader's Digest ® Trademark Reg. U.S. Pat. Off. Marca Registrada ISBN 0-88300-414-3

■ ■ ■ **Part 4**

Silver Edition

STORIES

4

The Seal That Thinks He's a Person
There were times when everyone thought André the seal was human. But could he find his way home across 200 miles of ocean? RDX 133

12 **The Amazing Philippe Petit** 🔈
It was no easy feat for this master of the high wire to step onto the slender cable stretched between the twin towers of one of the world's tallest buildings. RDX 134

22 **It All Adds Up**
A cash register without keys? That's not the only thing that is different about this marvelous machine. RDX 135

30 **A Bassoon of His Own** 🔈
Rolf's family learned far more than they expected from his strange-looking instrument. RDX 136

38 **Superstar of Metals**
The story of gold—its beauty, value, and uses—told in words and photographs. RDX 137

44 **The Guest**
A kindly old man shares some apples and a surprise visitor with Derry and her mother. RDX 138

🔈 Stories for which Audio Lessons are available.
RDX number indicates RDX card for that story.

52  **The Hong Kong Boat People**
When the author's small boat tips over in Hong Kong Harbor, he enters the world of the Hong Kong boat people.
RDX 139

60 Sold!
Who would pay $15 for a homemade cake? Mark and his father were surprised at the answer. RDX 140

66 Ice Caves in the Sky
Mount Rainier has some of the most unusual caves in the world. They are made of ice. RDX 141

72 "But We're Alive!"
Doris should have known better than to walk along the base of the cliff at high tide!
RDX 142

80 A Taste of Honey
Linda helps Jeff by teaching him about her very unusual hobby. RDX 143

88 Ancient People of the Rock
Who were these people who made beautiful baskets and built great cliff cities? RDX 144

Key Words

yolk
harbor
dock
aquarium

The Seal That Thinks He's a Person

by Lew Dietz

4

Harry Goodridge stood by the ocean at Rockport, Maine. His eyes scanned the Atlantic waters. He was waiting for a very special friend—a seal named André.

The day before, André had been put into the ocean near Boston, Massachusetts. That's almost 200 miles (321.86 kilometers) away. Could André find his way home?

Harry has studied ocean animals for a long time and knows that seals are among the smartest animals. But to Harry, André is more than smart. For over 13 years, André has seemed like a member of Harry's family.

Somehow André had lost his mother when he was very young. Harry had found the baby seal, built a tank for him in the cellar downstairs and filled the tank with water. Harry fed André egg yolk and milk until the little seal was old enough to eat fish.

As André grew up, Harry drove him to the harbor every day. There André could swim around in the water and play near the boats. Every night André climbed back into the car to go home.

By the third summer, André was too big for Harry to carry around. So the seal stayed in the harbor. There André waited for Harry to swim with him or feed him fish. As Harry worked and played with André, the seal learned more than 50 different tricks.

"That seal surprised me more each day," Harry told a friend. "Once, he nipped a button off my daughter's coat. The button sank. At first I was angry at André, but soon I forgot about it. Then, the next day, I went to the harbor. And what do you think? André swam underwater. When he came up again, he dropped the button right at my feet!"

André showed he could find things from a long way off. Once, while André was snoozing on the dock, Harry and a friend went far out into the bay in their boat. They began diving underwater.

"We were out of sight of the harbor," said Harry. "My friend turned around in the water. There was André! From four miles (6.44 kilometers) away, he knew exactly where to find us!"

It was clear that André liked people. And people liked him, too. Harry would ask him to

do tricks, such as leaping through hoops, shooting balls into baskets and stamping out fires with his flippers.

Because André thought he <u>was</u> a person, there was no fear of people in him. He would climb into small boats to take a nap and often sink them with his weight. Sometimes, just for fun, he would nip the oars on rowboats. One day he tipped over a canoe.

Harry built a special pen for André right on the water. Harry would come down to see André and take the seal out to swim and play in the harbor.

But during the long winter months, Harry was not always able to visit André.

The seal couldn't stay in a small pen all that time. If Harry let him swim free, André would tip over small fishing boats. The people in the boats would be dumped into the cold water.

That was it, thought Harry. He could not keep André out of trouble during the long winter months. So he took André to the aquarium in Boston. The seal would fit in nicely with the aquarium's many sea

creatures. In the spring, the aquarium people would bring André back to Maine by truck.

"No," said Harry, "we'll let him swim home to Rockport. I believe André can do it." That spring Harry went back down to Boston and slipped his seal friend into the water. "Go home, André, old-timer," he said.

Each day Harry waited by the sea, wondering if the seal would make it. The day after André left Boston, he was sighted off Kittery, Maine. Two days later, he was reported at Glen Cove, then at Owl's Head. Later he was seen taking a nap on a dock just a few miles from home.

Four days after André left Boston, Harry received a phone call. "André is at the harbor, asleep in a small boat," the caller said.

Harry drove fast to the shore. The tired old seal recognized the sound of Harry's car and opened his eyes. Harry gave him a fish and a loving pat on the head. Then André went back to sleep. He was back home at last.

Rockport
Glen Cove
Owl
Hea
Kittery
Gloucester
Boston

9

HARRY AND ANDRÉ *summary*

The sentences below sum up what happened in "The Seal That Thinks He's a Person." Write the letter of the missing word or words in each one.

André lost his ___.
  a. father   b. mother   c. sister

Harry Goodridge found André and took care of him. He kept the baby seal in a ___ in the cellar.
  a. box   b. cage   c. tank

Later André lived in the ___ in Rockport, Maine.
  a. woods   b. zoo   c. harbor

André learned to ___.
  a. walk on land   b. speak   c. do tricks

Then André had to spend the winter at the Boston aquarium. In the spring, he ___.
  a. swam back to Maine
  b. was taken home by truck
  c. went to live with a group of seals in Boston Harbor

☞ *134 • Best Score 5 • My Score* ___

GETTING TO KNOW SEALS *generalizations*

Some of the things seals do are listed on the next page. Underneath is a list of the things

André did. Write the numeral of each of André's actions in front of the matching sentence.

What Seals Do

___ They live on fish.
___ They live in the ocean.
___ They have good memories.
___ They like to play.
___ They can learn to do many new things.

What André Did

André . . .

1. lived in the harbor at Rockport.
2. remembered the button from the coat Harry's daughter had been wearing.
3. would eat the fish Harry gave him.
4. could do over 50 different tricks.
5. nipped the oars of rowboats.

☞ *166 • Best Score 5 • My Score* ___
All Best Scores 10 • All My Scores ___

OTHER ANIMALS   *comparison/contrast*

Why does André think he's a person? Can you think of other animals that understand people's words or actions? Explain.

The Amazing Philippe Petit

by Philippe Petit and John Reddy

Key Words

tightrope
juggler
cable
balancing

"I measure the wire with my eyes. I step carefully, putting one foot after the other with the greatest care. Slowly I put down my toes first. I slide the bottom of my foot along the wire. Then all the weight of my body is on the heel."

14

Philippe Petit, the daring tightrope walker and juggler, had just taken the first step on yet another of his high-wire walks. But this was no tightrope in a circus tent. It was a wire cable strung between the towers of what were, at that time, the tallest buildings in the world—the World Trade Center. Below Philippe lay the city of New York. People poured into the streets to watch. Others stared out office windows.

Back home in France, Philippe had dreamed of walking a wire between the towers of the World Trade Center. When he flew at last to New York City and saw the twin buildings, his mind was made up. He had to be up there. He would make his dream come true.

There was another problem besides the one of daring the wire itself. The World Trade Center was still being built. Philippe couldn't get very far with guards and workers all over the place. He wasn't going to give up, though. He made many visits to the building to learn all he could about it.

Later two of his friends from France flew in. They and Philippe made their plans.

Finally the big day came. Two friends started up the North Tower. Philippe and a friend named Heckel sneaked up the South Tower.

But trouble struck when they were stringing the heavy cable from one tower to the other. Says Philippe, "After the first few feet, I thought I would lose my fingers. The cable began to hum in my hands. Heckel and I couldn't hold it. It went swooshing into the emptiness in a giant U shape."

Their two friends in the North Tower needed tools to pull in the heavy cable. At last the wire was across. It was 6 a.m., broad daylight. It had taken them all night to string the cable across.

One hundred and ten stories above the ground, Philippe put together his balancing pole. "I am ready, even though the cable is not perfect and I have not set foot on a high wire for four months. It is a question of being a tightrope walker or not. I know that I will not be able to go backward. Therefore I am going to enjoy, with pleasure and fear, the role which I have chosen. For a few minutes, my entire life will be in my own hands.

"I push myself forward. The cable swings from top to bottom like a plucked string. It turns.

"Now I am more than halfway across. To have passed this point is to be filled with joy.

"As I near the North Tower, the wind tugs at my pole. I walk the rest of the distance, fighting off the wish to hurry. Many high-wire walkers have died on their last step, thinking they had made it.

"I put my toes on the tower. I am overcome with joy."

But now Philippe had to walk back. He watched the morning sun paint the thousands of glass windows in the World Trade Center

with silver. The Statue of Liberty looked no larger than a doll. A flock of pigeons drifted by, looking like tiny bits of paper. The people massed on the streets below looked like ants.

"As I near the other tower, I turn around for a third crossing. From this moment on, I will no longer be aware of the number of crossings. They will tell me later that I made seven crossings and that I stayed 45 minutes on the wire."

He was to call his last crossing "the most beautiful." In the middle of the wire, he dropped to one knee, the way all tightrope walkers do. There, at his feet, was all of New York City.

Philippe decided to end his walk there. He ran along the wire toward the tower and leaped onto the roof.

Philippe was the hero of New York—and the world. Newspapers and television wanted to tell about his amazing walk. Circuses wanted him to star in their shows. Philippe even performed free for the children of New York in the city's Central Park.

No matter what the future holds for Philippe, it is not money that makes him risk

his life on the high wire. When asked, "Why did you walk a high wire at the World Trade Center?" Philippe says, "When I see three oranges, I juggle. And when I see two towers, I walk."

COMPARE *figurative language*

Choose what the underlined word in each sentence reminds you of. Write its letter in the blank.

a. artist b. water c. bee d. hand

____ 1. People <u>poured</u> into the streets.
____ 2. "The cable began to <u>hum</u> in my hands."
____ 3. "As I near the North Tower, the wind <u>tugs</u> at my pole."
____ 4. The morning sun <u>painted</u> the windows in the World Trade Center with silver.

☞ *103 • Best Score 4 • My Score* ____

WHAT KIND OF PERSON? *sentence meaning*

Each main sentence tells you something about Philippe Petit. Circle the letter of one of the two sentences underneath that best describes Philippe.

1. *He made many visits to the buildings to learn all he could about them.*
    a. He plans his high-wire stunts well.
    b. He wants to put up a building.

2. *"I am ready, even though the cable is not perfect and I have not set foot on a high wire for four months."*

20

    a. He is afraid of walking on the wire.

    b. He is brave.

3. *"I walk the rest of the distance, fighting off the wish to hurry."*

    a. He is usually in a rush.

    b. He knows the dangers of the wire.

4. *"I am going to enjoy, with pleasure and fear, this role which I have chosen."*

    a. He is also a famous French actor.

    b. He loves the art of high-wire walking.

5. *"Heckel and I couldn't hold it."*

    a. The cable floated out of their hands.

    b. The cable was so heavy, it kept pulling out of their hands.

6. *"And when I see two towers, I walk."*

    a. He will continue to do high-wire feats because he loves to.

    b. He really wants to walk away from the dangers of the high wire.

⟝ 174 • Best Score 6 • My Score ____

All Best Scores 10 • All My Scores ____

IN HIS OWN WORDS   *points of view*

Why were Philippe Petit's own words used in some places instead of author John Reddy's? Do you think this way of telling Petit's story was a good idea? Why or why not?

IT ALL ADDS UP

Key Words

cashier
customer
checkout
cash register
computer

The cashier is about to pass this box of peas across the window and put it into the paper bag. The checkout system will do everything else.

by V. Elaine Smay

The supermarket cashier stood ready. The customer stacked food he was buying onto the checkout stand's top, which moved like a ramp. The cashier picked up each item for a moment and then stuffed it into a bag.

But wait a minute! There's a step missing. Do you know what it is?

The cashier wasn't touching the cash register.

The supermarket looks like any other. But its checkout stands are a bit unusual. More and more stores of all types are using the new checkout system.

This new system uses a new machine that can do all sorts of things. It can do math you can't do in your head. It will tell what a customer should pay for two T-shirts when the price for three is $5.35.

What do those strange lines and numbers mean? The lines help the machine find where the beginning, middle and end of the numbers are. The numbers describe the item for the computer. For example, look at the can above.

The little 0 at the left means the item came in a package or can of some kind.

The first five numbers at the bottom stand for the company that made the item.

The last five stand for the name and size of the item.

Scales at the checkout can weigh an item and add in its price.

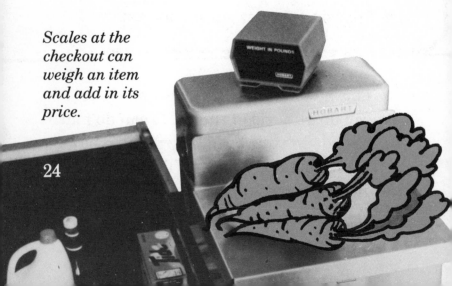

What does the cashier do? He or she simply pulls the food across a small window. The window is at the end of the checkout counter. On the side of the can or box or package is a row of light and dark lines. The lines have numbers. The checkout machine "reads" these lines and numbers when the item is passed across the window. The machine finds out what the item is and sends that message to a computer.

The computer knows all sorts of information about the item. The computer chooses the facts that might be needed and sends them back to the checkout machine. The machine flashes the name of the item and

If the lines and numbers aren't printed on the item, a store can use this handy little tool. It will stamp on the lines and numbers in just a few seconds.

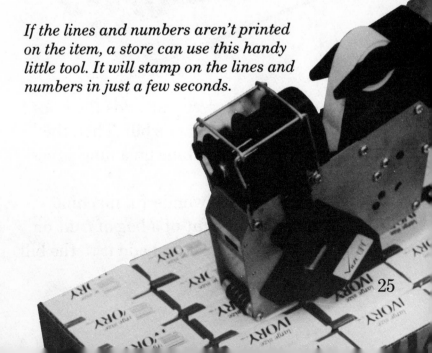

This machine flashes the name of the item and its price on the screen at the top. It also prints the bill for the customer. The keys aren't usually pressed by the cashier. They are there only in case a warning light tells her something is wrong with the system. Then it acts just like a cash register.

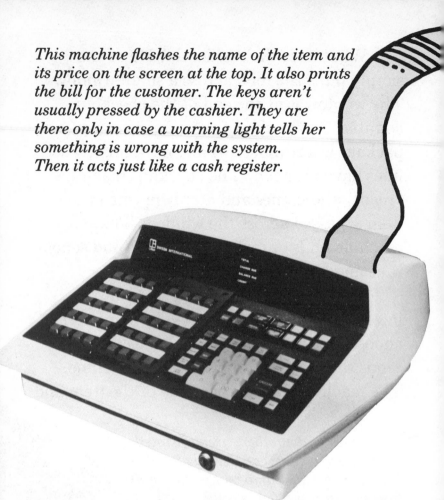

the price on a small screen and adds the price of that item to the customer's bill. Then the bill comes out of the machine on a long paper tape.

What else can this wonderful machine do? It can read the weight of a bag of fruit on a scale, figure out the cost and add it to the bill.

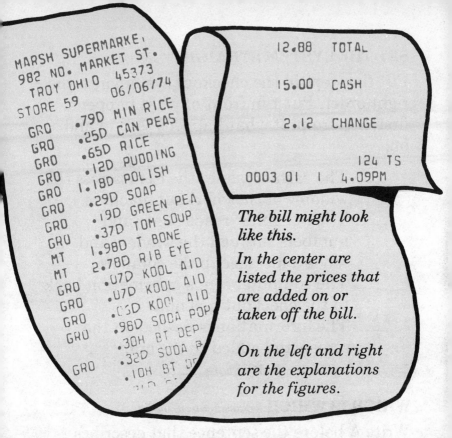

MARSH SUPERMARKE
982 NO. MARKET ST.
TROY OHIO 45373
STORE 59   06/06/74
GRO   .79D MIN RICE
GRO   .25D CAN PEAS
GRO   .65D RICE
GRO   .12D PUDDING
GRO   1.18D POLISH
GRO   .29D SOAP
GRO   .19D GREEN PEA
GRO   .37D TOM SOUP
MT   1.98D T BONE
MT   2.78D RIB EYE
GRO   .07D KOOL AID
GRO   .07D KOOL AID
GRO   .05D KOOL AID
GRO   .96D SODA POP
       .30H BT DEP
       .32D SODA
GRO   .10H BT D

12.88 TOTAL

15.00 CASH

2.12 CHANGE

124 TS
0003 01 1 4.09PM

The bill might look like this.

In the center are listed the prices that are added on or taken off the bill.

On the left and right are the explanations for the figures.

That's not all. The computer constantly gets information on which items are purchased and how fast they sell. It lets the store manager know when the store is running out of certain things. The manager can tell how many shoppers there were in the store at any time of the day.

It all adds up. Someday all supermarkets will probably use this speedy checkout system.

27

SET THE SYSTEM STRAIGHT *sequence*

Put the steps in the checkout system into the right order. Put 1 in front of what happens first, 2 in front of what happens second and so on.

_____ The cashier passes the item across the window of the checkout machine.

_____ The machine "reads" lines and numbers through the window and sends a message to the computer.

_____ The computer sends information back to the checkout machine.

_____ The information is flashed on the screen and added to the bill.

☞ *104 • Best Score 4 • My Score* _____

WHICH IS WHICH *classification/outline*

Write A before the sentence that describes the way the old checkout systems worked. Write B before the one that tells about the new checkout system. Write C before the one that talks about both the old and new systems.

_____ The cashier presses the cash register price keys.

_____ The checkout system depends on a computer.

28

____ The customer takes home food in a
paper bag.

☞ *49 • Best Score 3 • My Score* ____

THREE PLUSES   *main idea*

Put a plus sign (+) before the three most
important reasons the new checkout system is
good.

____ 1. fast
____ 2. doesn't need a cashier
____ 3. not expensive
____ 4. can do many things
____ 5. contains a lot of information

☞ *76 • Best Score 3 • My Score* ____
All Best Scores 10 • All My Scores ____

THE EASY WAY   *cause/effect*

Have you seen one of these new checkout
systems? Have you ever noticed the light and
dark lines on a can or box? Did you wonder
what the lines were for? How would this new
checkout system make life easier for <u>you</u>?
Explain.

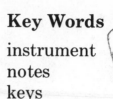

Key Words

instrument
notes
keys
director

A Bassoon of His Own

by Martha Prytula

Our son Rolf was
only 12 years old when
he introduced us to the
strangest instrument
in the school band. He
burst through the
front door and shouted,
"I've got a bassoon!"
He pointed to a large
black case.

30

Our eyes swung around from the television. "A what?" demanded the family.

"A baboon!" our five-year-old shrieked. "Rolf's got a baboon!"

Rolf corrected her immediately. "A bassoon, b-a-s-s-o-o-n. The band just bought it, and I'm the one who's been chosen to play it!"

Rolf zipped open the case. There, nestled in a soft green cloth, were four short black pipes. Each was studded with holes and silver keys.

He held up the thickest pipe. "This is the *butt*. The lowest notes come from its keys."

Carefully, proudly, he named each part as he put the bassoon together. On top of the butt went the *long joint*. From the side of it, a piece of wood called the *wing joint* stuck out. On top of the long joint was the *bell*. Last, Rolf slipped the *crook* and *mouthpiece* onto the wing joint. "I blow through this," he told

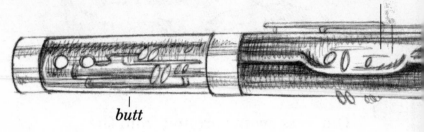

wing joint

butt

us. The bassoon now looked like a long black drainpipe.

"Can you play anything on it?" I asked.

"No, but I can give you an idea of what it sounds like." Rolf put his lips to the mouthpiece and blew, but no sound came out. He took a deep breath and tried again. This time the bassoon gave sort of a sneeze. Rolf gave it one more try. The instrument put out a low moan. B-O-O-M.

One of Rolf's brothers asked, "Is that it? It sounds like a moose."

Rolf was almost in tears. He tucked the bassoon under an arm and stomped out.

I turned to my family. "Look. Just because we don't know much about the instrument, we shouldn't make fun of it."

In the weeks that followed, I read all I could about the odd-looking instrument. I

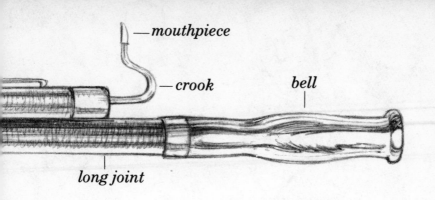

—*mouthpiece*

—*crook*

bell

long joint

found out that the bassoon is the most important low-pitched instrument in a band. But it is also <u>very</u> difficult to play.

Meanwhile, from behind Rolf's bedroom door came the squawks and groans of what was supposed to be music. One day he came home from a music lesson at school. I'd never seen him so upset.

He complained, "The band director expects too much of me. You can tell him I'm quitting."

"If you're sure you want to quit, <u>you</u> call the director and say so."

At first Rolf didn't want to do it. Finally he said, "Okay, I'll tell him."

But Rolf never did. The next week, he lugged his bassoon off to the lesson as usual. All winter long, the squeaks and moans sounded throughout the house.

At last it was time for the Spring Festival, the contest for young musicians. That year the festival ran for five days. Five hundred music students were trying to win prize money. Of course, Rolf didn't have much of a chance. But he was certainly going to try.

The first morning of the festival found me sitting with the other nail-nibbling parents. As Rolf began his piece, a man behind me whispered, "What sort of instrument is that?"

"It's a bassoon," I admitted. I felt like hiding.

"What a perfectly beautiful sound!"

So I sat up and listened. It was the first time I had truly heard the bassoon, and it <u>was</u> lovely.

Rolf grew up to be a musician and became one of the best bassoonists in the country. But whether he did well or not, we, his parents, learned something. We realized we should help our children do the things that are most important to them. With our love, they can reach for their own star. For a drainpipe, that bassoon turned out to be a pretty good teacher.

MISSING SOMETHING? *signals/antecedents*

Each contraction in slanted letters in the sentences below is a short way of saying <u>two</u> words. In each blank, write the numeral of the complete word that was shortened in the contraction. You will use one numeral twice.

1. are
2. am
3. have
4. not
5. is

___ "*I've* got a bassoon!"

___ "You can tell him *I'm* quitting."

___ "Just because we *don't* know anything about the instrument, we shouldn't make fun of it."

___ "If *you're* sure you want to quit, you call the director."

___ I was sorry I *hadn't* called the director.

___ "*It's* a bassoon."

205 • *Best Score 6* • *My Score* ___

WORD PICTURES *graphics*

Write the letter of the picture that stands for the word the author used in the story. You will <u>not</u> use one letter.

36

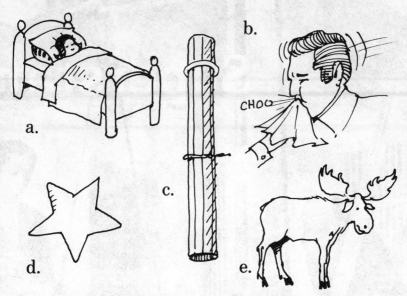

a.

b.

CHOO

c.

d.

e.

1. "Is that it? It sounds like a ___."
2. This time the bassoon gave sort of a ___.
3. The bassoon now looked like a long black ___.
4. With our love, they can reach for their own ___.

111 • Best Score 4 • My Score ___
All Best Scores 10 • All My Scores ___

WORDS AND SOUNDS   *figurative language*

What does a bassoon sound like? Make up words that describe its sounds. Try to make those sounds with your voice. Do the same with other musical instruments.

Superstar

of Metals

by Ernest O. Hauser

Key Words

jewelry
gold leaf
mines, miner
explosives
karat

It seems to last forever. It cannot be destroyed by air, wind or water. It can be melted down over and over again to be made into new shapes.

Many people all over the world want to own it. It is worth a lot of money. It has many uses. And it is one of the most lovely metals on earth. The metal, of course, is gold.

Where does gold come from? It is found in three places. It is trapped in rock above and below ground. Grains of gold lie loose in streams or in streambeds where water used to flow. And gold is found in small amounts in seawater.

Most countries print paper money or make cheap metal coins. But many of them keep supplies of gold. The gold shows people how much the coins and paper money are worth.

39

Most people are used to seeing gold in jewelry. But gold is used for lots of other things besides rings, tie clips and necklaces. There are gold pen points. Dentists sometimes put gold fillings in teeth. People make *gold leaf* by melting gold and cutting it into square pieces. These pieces are hammered till they are thin enough to shine light through. Then the gold leaf is put on dishes, glass, picture frames, buildings and

lettering on glass doors and windows. Gold is even used on astronauts' spacesuits. Gold can protect the astronauts from harmful rays from space.

Gold has charmed people for thousands of years. Are we likely to run out of gold after all this time? No. There seems to be plenty of gold in the gold mines that are still open. There will probably be enough gold to charm people for the next 6000 years.

A karat is the way people measure how much gold is in a piece of jewelry. The number 24 stamped on gold stands for 24 karats. That means the item is all gold. If 18 appears, it tells people the item is 18 parts gold and six parts some other metal. (Eighteen plus six equals 24.)

Drilling Holes in a Gold Mine. When gold is embedded in underground rock, mines have to be dug. This miner is in a mine tunnel under the earth. He is drilling long holes into the rock. Next he will put explosives into the holes. The explosives will blow apart the rock. Then the gold can be easily taken away.

PROSPECT FOR GOLD   *supporting details*

Check (✔) three places people find gold.

____ 1. seawater
____ 2. space
____ 3. air
____ 4. trees
____ 5. rocks
____ 6. streambeds

🔑 *82 • Best Score 3 • My Score* ____

IN PRAISE OF GOLD   *author's purpose*

Check (✔) four things mentioned by the author to show you that gold is useful.

____ 1. one of the most beautiful metals on earth
____ 2. pen points
____ 3. astronauts' spacesuits
____ 4. gold mines
____ 5. gold leaf
____ 6. tooth fillings

🔑 *122 • Best Score 4 • My Score* ____

PRECIOUS PARAGRAPHS   *paragraph meaning*

Each main sentence on the next page could be the beginning sentence in a paragraph. Circle the letter of one of the two sentences underneath that tells about the main sentence.

1. Where does gold come from?
   a. It cannot be destroyed by air, wind or water.
   b. It is found in rock above and below ground.

2. Gold is used for many other things besides jewelry.
   a. People put gold leaf on dishes, glass, picture frames, buildings and the lettering on glass doors and windows.
   b. A *karat* is the way people measure how much gold is in a piece of jewelry.

3. Gold has charmed people for thousands of years.
   a. Most countries print paper money or make cheap metal coins.
   b. Are we likely to run out of gold after all this time?

⊶ 42 · Best Score 3 · My Score ——
All Best Scores 10 · All My Scores ——

PRECIOUS GIFTS   *appreciation*

What beautiful things has nature given us besides gold? Are any of them worth a lot of money, or are some of them desired for other reasons? Explain.

The Guest

by J. J. A. McConney

Key Word
guest
porch

"There's the sign, Mom! Apples!"

I glanced at the wooden sign. It said that one of the farmers had apples for sale. I nodded to my daughter Derry and turned the car down the bumpy dirt road.

Soon we arrived at a brown and weather-beaten house that sat on a hilltop.

"This can't be the place," I said to Derry. "It looks empty."

Just then a screen door on the side of the house slammed, and a man came around the corner of the porch. He was tall and old and twisted, just like one of the big shade trees.

"We're looking for apples," I said to him. "We saw the sign down on the highway."

"That's the Bensons' sign," he told us. "They had to go away a few days ago."

"Then we won't be able to buy any apples," said Derry sadly.

The old man slowly smiled. "I don't have enough apples to sell, but I could give you a basketful."

The old man led Derry and me around to the neatly swept back porch. He opened the creaking screen door and went into the kitchen. Derry darted in after him. She had spotted his dog.

I followed them inside and heard the old
man say, "My dog's name is Sam." Sam
leaned his graying head against my
daughter's knee and then turned so that she
could scratch his ears.

The old man got a basket and put it next
to a heap of apples that was on the table. He
picked out the best ones for us and put them
in the basket. Then he spoke again. "If you
can wait just a few minutes, there will be
something your daughter might like to see."

The old man opened a can of dog food
and spooned the contents onto a tin plate. He

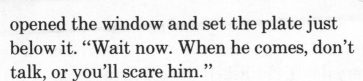

opened the window and set the plate just below it. "Wait now. When he comes, don't talk, or you'll scare him."

"When who comes?" Derry wanted to know.

The old man just smiled a secret smile and put a finger to his lips to quiet her. This visitor was to be his surprise. We all sat in silence.

We didn't have long to wait. A small shape flitted through the air and landed on the kitchen windowsill. It peered at us with unblinking yellow eyes.

"Oh!" gasped Derry. "It's an owl."

The brown-and-gray bird turned his head toward Derry. But he did not fly away. Instead, he looked at us carefully.

When the bird decided we meant him no harm, he hopped onto the counter and started eating the dog food. We watched, not daring to move. He ate quickly and neatly. He stopped now and then to gaze at us.

When he finished, he snapped one side of his beak and then the other against the dish. He returned to the window, bowed twice and flew off.

I looked at Derry and saw she was as charmed by the bird as I was. "Does he come every day?" she asked the old man.

"He comes every day at this time. I'd really miss him if he didn't come."

"If you could catch him," suggested Derry, "you could keep him."

The old man smiled and gently shook his head. It was a smile for me. The smile was saying, "It can't be done. You and I know— and she will learn. You can't chain someone

or something you love to you. We love, and we let go. There is no other way."

His smile told me all that. But to Derry he put it another way. "Old Sam is family. But that owl, now, he's a guest. It wouldn't be kind to do that to a guest, would it?"

"No," admitted Derry. She gathered up the basket of apples and hugged it. I tried to pay for them, but the old man would take no money from us.

The old man walked us to our car. Sam followed, his tail waving good-bye. Once we had said farewell and started back home, the dirt road was like an old friend. We reached the highway as the last glow of daylight slipped from the trees.

Derry bit into one of the sweet, juice-filled apples. She thought hard as her teeth crunched. Then she asked me, "How do you know who's a guest and who's family?"

I answered as best I could. "Sam showed he was part of that man's family because he stayed and made it his home. But that owl came just to say hello and have a bite to eat. I guess everyone is a guest until he or she tells you otherwise."

PICTURE THIS *story elements*

What words did the author use to help you see each person or thing listed below? Write the numerals in the blanks.

1. the house
2. the porch
3. the old man
4. the apples
5. the owl's eyes

___ sweet, juice-filled
___ brown, weather-beaten
___ tall, old and twisted
___ neatly swept
___ unblinking, yellow

☞ 165 • *Best Score 5* • *My Score* ___

REPHRASE THE PHRASE *phrase meaning*

Match the underlined phrase in each sentence below with its meaning. Write the numerals in the blanks.

1. familiar   2. quietly   3. to sell

___ It said that one of the farmers had apples <u>for sale.</u>
___ We all sat <u>in silence.</u>
___ Once we had said farewell and started back home, the dirt road was <u>like an old friend.</u>

☞ 54 • *Best Score 3* • *My Score* ___

THE OLD MAN'S SMILE *paragraph meaning*

Read the two paragraphs on pages 48 and 49 that begin with, "The old man smiled and gently shook his head," and end with, "It wouldn't be kind to do that to a guest, would it?"

Draw an apple (🍎) next to the two sentences below that sum up the meaning of the two paragraphs.

___ 1. If you love someone, you have to let that person have his or her freedom.

___ 2. Every person and animal would really like to run away from home.

___ 3. The old man liked telling secrets.

___ 4. A person or animal stays because it wants to, not because it is forced to.

⎯22 • Best Score 2 • My Score ___
All Best Scores 10 • All My Scores ___

FAMILY OR COMPANY? *points of view*

Do you have a pet? If you do, is it part of the family or a guest? Explain. If you don't, what kind of pet would you like to have? Would it be part of the family or a guest? Explain.

The Hong Kong

by Frank Robertson

Whoosh! The wind began to tip my small boat. Suddenly I was swimming in Hong Kong Harbor. But before I knew it, I saw several smiling faces looking down at me. Soon I was lifted onto Mr. and Mrs. Chan's *junk* (Chinese boat).

I'd heard of these boat people. They are known as the Tanka. They live on junks in Hong Kong Harbor. They have all they need in their boat world.

Mr. and Mrs. Chan, their parents, their eight children, their own brothers and sisters

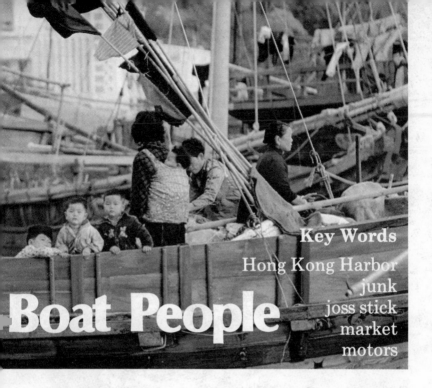

Key Words

Hong Kong Harbor
junk
joss stick
market
motors

Boat People

with their children, and a frisky chow puppy were all living on their junk. Mrs. Chan took me downstairs so I could dry off. She gave me hot tea. Down below, I saw the kitchen, bedrooms and living area.

Grandma Chan began to tell me of old Tanka beliefs. "See this stick," she said, pointing to the *joss stick* with the number on it. "I use sticks like this one before every trip we take in the junk. The numbers on the joss sticks tell me whether we will have good luck or if we should stay home."

Mr. Chan spoke. "Years ago, we were caught in a terrible storm. Grandma still thinks her joss sticks saved us from that storm, but I know that it was my sailing skill that saved us! Today we can find out from listening to the weather report if there will be a storm. We don't have to use lucky sticks to find out!"

Grandma ignored her son's new ideas and went on to tell me more about old Tanka beliefs. "We never turn an empty rice bowl upside down. This could mean our junk would turn over, too," she explained.

"You should rest now, while it's quiet," Mrs. Chan told me. "Tonight we must fish." Most Tanka families fish every night except on their two holidays, the Chinese New Year and the Dragon Boat Festival. Very early the next morning, they go to the market to sell their fish.

Not all Tanka people fish, though. In one part of the harbor are lines of boats that do not sail from the docks to which they are tied. When someone wants to go to a restaurant or ice-cream seller, he or she sails up the waterway "streets" formed by the lines of boats.

But the lives of the Tanka people are slowly changing. Junks now have motors and are easier to handle, so not so many people are required to sail the boats. In the olden days, children helped sail their families' boats, too. But today many Tanka children go to school instead. The schools are on land. And Tanka people have begun to marry people who live on land. Many of the boat people have moved into homes on land.

The change to living on land is not always easy for the Tanka. It usually takes a

few weeks for them to get used to sleeping in a bed that does not rock.

Yes, many boat people are happiest living on junks in Hong Kong Harbor. Thank goodness they were there to help me when my boat tipped over!

THE BOAT PEOPLE *skimming*

Skim the story to find the answers to the questions below. Circle the letter of the correct answer.

1. Where do most of the Tanka live?
   a. in caves   b. on junks   c. in houses

2. Who lives on the junks?
   a. mainland people   b. sailors
   c. whole families

3. When do the Tanka do their fishing?
   a. at night   b. Chinese New Year
   c. Dragon Boat Festival

4. Why are fewer people needed to sail junks?
   a. There are too many storms.
   b. Junks now have motors.
   c. The government isn't letting as many Tanka catch fish.

90 · Best Score 4 · My Score ___

TANKA BELIEFS *fact/opinion*

Check (✔) the two sentences that tell about old Tanka beliefs.

The Tanka . . .
___ 1. go ashore when a storm is coming.
___ 2. eat breakfast after they go to market.
___ 3. have some junks that never move.

_____ 4. use joss sticks to tell if their boats will have good or bad luck.

_____ 5. like a bed that rocks them to sleep.

_____ 6. think an upside-down rice bowl means their boat will turn over.

⌐∽ 40 · *Best Score 2 · My Score* _____

THE TANKA WORLD   *summary*

Draw waves (∿∿) next to the four sentences below that sum up the <u>most important</u> ideas in the story.

_____ 1. Mrs. Chan gave the author tea.

_____ 2. The Tanka have everything they need in their boat world.

_____ 3. The author learned many things about the Tanka's way of life.

_____ 4. Mr. Chan listens to the weather report before he goes fishing.

_____ 5. Many boat people are happiest living on junks in Hong Kong Harbor.

_____ 6. The Tanka are learning new ways.

⌐∽ 122 · *Best Score 4 · My Score* _____

All Best Scores 10 · All My Scores _____

LIFE STYLES   *comparison/contrast*

How is life on a Tanka junk like yours? How is it different?

SOLD!

Key Words

auction
Cub Scout
frosting
masterpiece

60

by Margie Nuremberg

Mark and his father were going to bake a cake. Mark took the things he needed from the kitchen shelf and checked his list to be sure he had remembered everything.

"This will be the very best cake at the father-and-son auction," Mark thought. Then he called, "Dad, we'll need two bowls, two pans and a wooden spoon." Since these things were kept high on a shelf, Mark couldn't reach them, even if he stood on a stool.

Mark's Cub Scout pack was holding a cake auction, and they hoped to get enough money to fix up their playground.

Each Scout and his father were to bake a cake. These cakes would then be sold at the auction. People would bid against each other for each cake. Whoever paid the most money for a cake would win it. He or she would get something that was good to eat and fun to look at!

Step by step, Mark read to his father from the cookbook. His father did as Mark told him. When they were finished, their cake was ready for the oven.

They watched TV while their cake was baking. Then the timer on the stove rang, and Dad took the cake from the oven.

Now came the fun part. Mark had bowls of colored frosting ready. Together, he and Dad planned how their cake would look. Then they spread blue frosting all over the top of the cake.

Mark gently set a small, round cake on top of this sea of frosting. "This will be the island," Mark said to his father. He frosted the island in a sandy color. Next they put in trees and bushes with green frosting and little fish with gold frosting. And last, Dad added some whitecaps to the sea waves. "A real masterpiece! It looks like a painting good enough to eat," he said, and they both laughed.

Dad had to work on Monday, the day of the cake auction. All day long, he wondered if someone had purchased their cake. Finally his wife phoned him at his job.

"Earl, I have great news! Everyone thought the cake was fantastic. It was the best one at the auction. It sold for $15!"

"Fifteen dollars! But whoever paid that much for a cake?" he asked.

"Well . . . I did," she replied.

THE CAKE MAKERS *signals/antecedents*

In each sentence underneath the picture, one word is underlined. In the blanks before each sentence, write the numeral of the person or persons referred to.

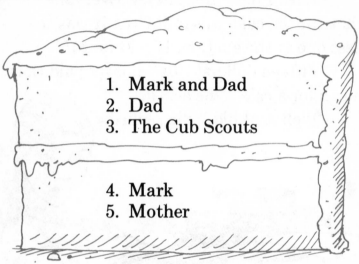

1. Mark and Dad
2. Dad
3. The Cub Scouts

4. Mark
5. Mother

____ <u>He</u> checked his list to be sure he had remembered everything.

____ <u>They</u> hoped to get enough money to fix up their playground.

____ Then <u>they</u> spread blue frosting all over the top of the cake.

____ All day long, <u>he</u> wondered if someone had bought their masterpiece.

____ "Well . . . <u>I</u> did."

🔑 *167 • Best Score 5 • My Score ____*

PLAIN CAKE? *fact/opinion*

Write 1 next to each sentence below that is a fact. Write 2 next to each one that is an opinion.

_____ Since these things were kept high on a shelf, Mark couldn't reach them, even if he stood on a stool.

_____ "This will be the very best cake at the father-and-son auction."

_____ "A real masterpiece!"

_____ Mark's Cub Scout pack was holding a cake auction to get money.

_____ Now came the fun part.

131 • Best Score 5 • My Score _____
All Best Scores 10 • All My Scores _____

WHAT'S SO FUNNY? *story elements*

What made this story funny? Would the article have been as funny if someone other than Mark's mother had bought the cake? How would you bake and frost a cake if you wanted it to sell at an auction?

Key Words

caves
Mount Rainier
volcano
dormant
craters
grotto

Ice Caves

Imagine that you and your mountain climbing friends have just reached the top of Mount Rainier (ruh-NEER), one of the highest mountains in the United States. You see a dark patch in the snow. When you get close to this dark patch, you realize that it is a hole. Steamy, awful-smelling gases come from it.

This hole is actually the entrance to an unusual kind of cave. You notice that the walls and ceiling are solid ice. The floor is dirt. The air is damp and foggy. The ceiling drips, drips, drips water.

This is an ice cave. It is one of the many ice caves of Mount Rainier. They are the highest known caves in the world.

Mount Rainier is more than a mountain. It's a volcano as well. But it is a *dormant*

Adapted by permission from <u>National Parks & Conservation Magazine</u>, March 1975. Copyright © 19
by National Parks & Conservation Association.

in the Sky

by Eugene P. Kiver

(sleeping, quiet) volcano. So mountain climbers can safely climb to its snowy top.

Even though the volcano is dormant, it gives off steamy, hot gases. The gases melt some of the ice underneath the snow. In this way, the ice caves are formed.

There is still plenty of snow above the ice cave roofs. Mount Rainier usually gets about 40 feet (12.19 meters) of snow each year. Someone discovered a red woolen glove hanging from the roof of an ice cave. The glove must have been dropped on the snow 30 or 40 years before. The glove slowly sank with the melting ice. It came out at last in the cave roof after working its way through 300 feet (91.44 meters) of snow and ice.

The top of Mount Rainier has two *craters*. A crater is a bowl-shaped hole out of which hot rock, smoke and ash come when a volcano is active. But Mount Rainier is dormant, so its two craters are dead. They have been covered by snow.

People reach the ice caves by going into openings in the craters. There are about 16 of these entrances in the east crater and nine in the smaller west crater.

Some of the tunnels leading to the caves are low and narrow. But the main tunnels that lead around the crater are large. Some parts of the main east crater tunnel are three stories high and at least twice as wide.

A special type of ice cave is the *grotto*. A grotto is a huge, roomlike cave. The Lake Grotto in the west crater even has a small lake in one corner.

People are still studying the ice caves. They may find new caves. They may find out more about how Mount Rainier was formed. And if the ice ever starts to melt very fast, it will be a warning that the dormant volcano is waking up.

FROZEN PICTURES *vocabulary*

Match each picture with a word that describes it. Write the letters in the blanks.

a. crater   d. dormant
b. volcano   e. grotto
c. tunnel

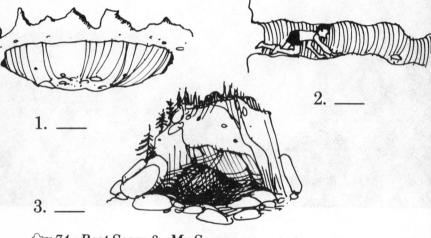

1. ___

2. ___

3. ___

🔑 74 • *Best Score 3 • My Score* ___

THE COLD FACTS *supporting details*

Underline the word or words that best complete each sentence.

1. Mount Rainier is one of the (a. highest mountains, b. most active volcanos, c. best ski slopes) in the United States.

2. It usually gets about (a. 4, b. 14, c. 40) feet of snow each year.

3. At Mount Rainier's top are (a. homes for mountain climbers, b. hot rock, smoke and ash, c. two dead craters).

4. People reach the ice caves by (a. chopping away at the ice and snow, b. entering openings in the crater, c. following tunnels that lead upward from the bottom of the mountain).

🔑89 • *Best Score 4* • *My Score* ____

ONE, TWO, THREE   *sequence*

Put the steps that create ice caves into the correct order. Write 1 before what happens first, 2 before what happens next and 3 before what happens last.

____ Ice is melted by hot gases underneath.
____ Snow changes to ice.
____ Snow falls from the sky.

🔑54 • *Best Score 3* • *My Score* ____
All Best Scores 10 • *All My Scores* ____

FUN BUT DANGEROUS   *comparison/contrast*

How are the ice caves like regular caves? How are they different? How could a cave be dangerous? What things should a person know and do before going into a cave?

71

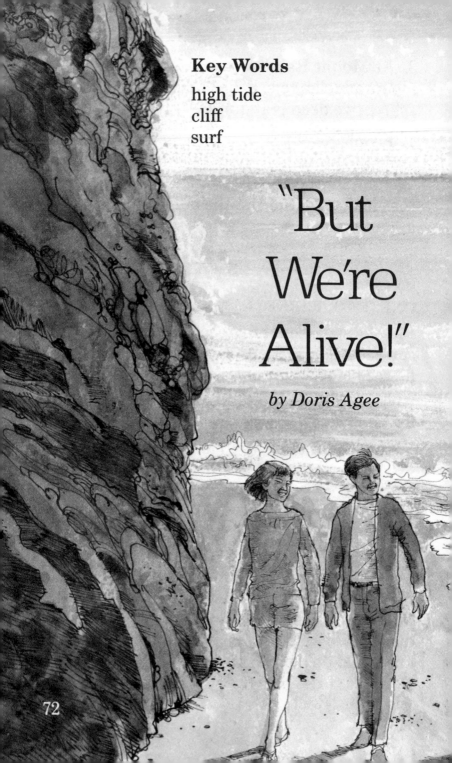

Key Words

high tide
cliff
surf

"But We're Alive!"

by Doris Agee

72

I will never forget that day. Two friends, Don and Lee, came to visit me in California. I drove them along the shore road to show them the beach. We got out of the car.

I should have noticed that it would soon be high tide. It would be time for the water to rise.

Don, Lee and I walked down to a large cliff with a flat top. Its dark brown sides rose from the sand. We walked along the front of it to see what lay beyond.

Beyond the cliff lay the ocean. The sand seemed more than wide enough for walking. Then I noticed that the rocks were wet to a point well above our heads. That was how far the water came up at high tide.

I was just about to mention the waterline when we all saw the huge wave foaming at us. There was nowhere to run. So we braced ourselves by leaning back against the rock.

The powerful wave went beneath me, rode me straight up the rock and then fell back on itself. Suddenly I was being turned and twisted and thrown down, again and again.

Within moments, I was far out at sea. I looked up and saw a huge wave rising. In the next instant, I was being carried ahead of the wave. I was going to be dashed to pieces against the cliff!

But the wave took me only to a point just short of the beach. Don was standing in the surf nearby. His hands reached toward me.

Then I felt myself moving with great speed, back into the deep water. The wave that had carried me almost to safety was now taking me out to sea.

Again there was the helpless turning and twisting and the gasping for air. Once more, a wave took me nearly to the beach, only to drag me away again.

Then a huge wave broke over my head. I can't remember what happened too clearly after that. Once, I heard someone yell, "Hold on! I've got you!" But the voice sounded strange and far away, and I felt no hand on mine.

Later on, I learned the voice had been Don's. The wave had brought me straight to him. He had grabbed at my limp hand, but it slipped from his as the surf tore me back into deep water.

Suddenly I found myself face down on the beach. Don crawled to me, grabbed my hand and collapsed on the sand at my side. But neither of us could move. I knew I would be swept into the sea for the final time.

Then Lee was there. Somehow she got Don to his feet, and the two of them pulled me up. Stumbling, falling, crawling, we fought to get beyond the rocks. At last we fell in a wet heap onto the safe, dry sand. We stayed there for a long time, not moving, not speaking. We just held onto one another.

People gathered around us now. Someone said, "I live over in that small house. I've seen a lot of people caught where you were. Most of them don't make it back."

Suddenly we were all talking at once. We counted our losses—my wallet, Don's ring, Lee's watch. Yes, we counted what we'd lost. And each time we ended with, "But we're <u>alive!</u>"

GRAINS OF SAND *skimming*

Skim the story for answers to the sentences below. Draw a grain of sand (✑) around the letter of the missing word or words.

1. Doris Agee lived in ____.
    a. Hawaii   b. California   c. Florida

2. The color of the cliff was ____.
    a. black   b. steel gray   c. dark brown

3. Doris and her friends were trapped between ____.
    a. the ocean and the cliff
    b. the ocean and the beach
    c. the cliff and the shore road

4. When Doris, Lee and Don reached the safety of the beach, they ____.
    a. had to be taken to a hospital
    b. fell on the sand for quite a while
    c. felt better in a few seconds

⚷ 90 • *Best Score 4* • *My Score* ____

SUPER SURF *sentence meaning*

Check (✔) the four sentences that show the power of the surf.

____ 1. I drove them along the shore road.
____ 2. Suddenly I was being turned and twisted and thrown down.

_____ 3. The sand seemed more than wide enough for walking.

_____ 4. Within moments, I was far out at sea.

_____ 5. Don was standing in the surf nearby.

_____ 6. I can't remember what happened.

_____ 7. I heard waves crashing behind me.

_____ 8. A wave took me nearly to the beach, only to drag me away again.

☞124 • *Best Score 4* • *My Score* _____

FLOW OF THOUGHT   *main idea*

Check (✔) the two most important ideas in the story.

_____ 1. People don't realize how important life is until their lives are in danger.

_____ 2. People should dress in swimming clothes when walking along a beach.

_____ 3. Accidents often happen in the same place.

_____ 4. True friends help you when you need them most.

☞22 • *Best Score 2* • *My Score* _____

All Best Scores 10 • *All My Scores* _____

LOOKING AT THINGS   *points of view*

Why do you think the author used the title "But We're Alive!" for her article? What other titles might she have used?

Key Words

honey, honeycomb
beehives
swarm
larvae

A Taste

Jeff was sitting in science class. "This month we're going to study animals," said Mr. Peron. "Each of you should select an animal and find out all you can about it. In one month, report to the class and tell us what you discovered."

Then the bell rang, and the students grabbed their books and crowded outside. Jeff moaned, "I don't know what animal to study."

"You could study my pets," suggested Linda. "They're quite different. Why don't you come home with me and see?"

Linda led Jeff to the toolshed behind her house. "I keep my gear here," she said. "I raise bees."

Jeff was surprised. "Why?"

"For honey, of course. And they're fun to watch. But you have to wear special clothes if you're around a beehive."

When Jeff finished putting on all the

# of Honey

by Jacqueline D. Kinghorn

things he needed, Linda took him out to one of her beehives. As she took off each section of the hive and explained its use, she sprayed it with smoke. In a minute or so, Jeff noticed that the bees seemed sleepy.

Linda gently picked up one of the bees. "This bee is a *worker*. Workers take care of the queen bee and her eggs. They also build the nest and guard the entrance.

"They're the ones you'll see out in the fields gathering nectar and pollen from the flowers. The pollen collects in baskets on their rear legs."

"But why do they collect pollen and nectar?"

"For food. They also turn the nectar into honey."

Linda put the worker back and lifted up another bee. "This type of bee is called a *drone*. You can see it's fat and has lots of hair all over its body.

"The drones are the only males in the hive. They have no sting. One of them will mate with the queen once so that she will lay worker eggs for the rest of her life. But that's a drone's only job."

Linda pointed to a bee that was surrounded by lots of other bees. "That bee is the queen. You can see she's bigger than the other bees.

"Every beehive has to have a queen. She has only one job, but it's a very important one. She lays the eggs.

"I check my hives every week or ten days," Linda explained. "I want to see how much honey the bees are producing. And I have to make sure they have enough room to raise their young. If the bees are too crowded, they will swarm."

"What's that?" asked Jeff.

"When there are too many bees in a hive, the queen stops laying eggs. Several days later, the queen and many of the workers swarm. They fly like a black cloud and find a new home. A few workers remain in the old hive. They take care of the tiny wormlike larvae that grow from the eggs. These larvae

BEEKEEPER'S OUTFIT

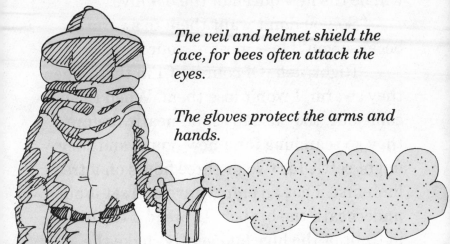

The veil and helmet shield the face, for bees often attack the eyes.

The gloves protect the arms and hands.

A smoker is used to quiet the bees without hurting them. It makes their bodies bend so that the bees can't sting.

The sleeves and bottoms of the pants are pulled in snugly so that the bees won't crawl up the arms or legs.

Beekeepers often wear a suit and boots to stop the bees from stinging through their clothing. After people work around bees for a season or two, their bodies get used to being stung. The stings don't swell anymore. They wear just a veil, a long-sleeved shirt and pants tucked into their boots. They don't even have to wear gloves.

will turn into adult bees. One of these larvae will be the new queen of the old hive."

"So you don't want them to swarm because you'll lose most of your bees."

"Right, Jeff. Of course, if I'm there when they swarm, I won't lose them. When the bees come out, they usually land nearby before they go searching for a new home, and they might settle for two or three hours on a tree limb first. I get an empty hive and set it out underneath the branch. I spread a cloth out in front of the hive and gently shake the branch. The bees fall or land on the cloth and then head for my new hive."

"How do you collect the honey?" asked Jeff.

"Usually I put the honeycomb in a machine called an *extractor*. It's a barrel or tank with a wire basket inside. I put the honeycomb into the extractor and turn the handle on top. The basket spins, and as it does, the honey flies from the comb. Then I'll have just the honey."

"I can't believe there's so much to know about bees," said Jeff. "I'll have plenty to report to the class next month!"

THE BEEHIVE

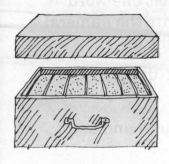

The outer cover *and* inner cover *keep out rain and snow.*

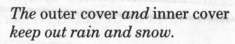

Honey is stored in one or more extracting supers. *When they get full, the beekeeper puts new ones in their place.*

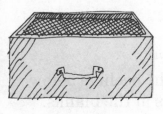

The holes in the screen of the queen excluder *are too small to let the queen through. She must stay in the hive body and lay her eggs there. So the workers have to store their extra honey in the super above. An excluder gives the beekeeper more honey.*

There are ten frames with wire grids in each hive body. *Pressing the wire into the beeswax helps the bees make honeycombs. The queen lays her eggs here.*

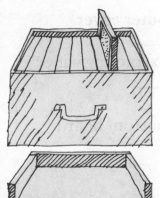

The bottom board *is like a floor. It has an entrance for the workers.*

The hive stand *keeps the hive off the ground so rain or pests won't get in easily.*

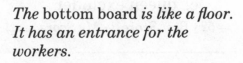

KNOW YOUR BEES *signals/antecedents*

Each of the sentences below has one word underlined. In each blank, write the numeral of the kind of bee being described.

1. queen   2. worker   3. drone

____ <u>She</u> lays the eggs.
____ <u>It</u> takes care of the queen and her eggs.
____ <u>It</u> has no sting.

🔑 55 • *Best Score 3* • *My Score* ____

THE BEEHIVE *classification/outline*

The names of three parts of the beehive below are missing. Write their letters in the blanks.

outer cover

____
extracting super

____
bottom board

a. hive body
b. inner cover
c. queen excluder

🔑 52 • *Best Score 3* • *My Score* ____

BEEKEEPER AT WORK *inferences*

Pretend you are a beekeeper. Circle the letter of the correct answers.

What would you do if . . .

you wanted to check your hives without getting stung?
    a. use a smoker
    b. keep on the top cover

you wanted more honey?
    a. bring in more drones
    b. put in a queen excluder

you wanted to separate the honey from the comb?
    a. use an extractor
    b. press the honey out with your hive tool

you saw your bees were getting ready to swarm?
    a. feed them pollen
    b. add a new hive body to give them more room

⟜ *84 • Best Score 4 • My Score* ____
All Best Scores 10 • All My Scores ____

HOBBIES   *comparison/contrast*

Do you have a hobby? Tell a little about it and how you became interested in it. If you don't have a hobby, would you like to take up one? Why or why not?

Ancient People of the Rock

by Donald G. Pike

It was a bitterly cold December day in 1888. Two cowhands were searching for lost cattle. The sky was heavy with snow. An icy wind blew a curtain of light snow around the two men. They stopped their horses at the edge of rock that overlooked the canyon below.

Suddenly the wind shifted. Now the cowhands could see clearly into the canyon. They could hardly believe what they saw. The empty rooms and towers of an old Anasazi (an-ah-SAH-zee) Indian city stared back at the two men. The buildings had been built right into the side of the canyon!

The cowhands rode down into the canyon. They looked up at the stone houses that had been empty for several hundred years. Inside the buildings, the men found clay pots, a stone ax and the bones of several people.

By luck, those cowhands had found Mesa Verde (MAY-sah VER-day), one of the many towns and cities built by the Anasazi. *Anasazi* is a Navajo (NAV-uh-hoh) Indian word meaning "the Ancient Ones." The Anasazi lived in the southwest section of the United States for about 1300 years. They had built great cities long before Christopher Columbus was born.

The land on which the Anasazi lived was very dry. There wasn't much rainfall during the year. So the Anasazi searched for the water they needed to stay alive. When they found a good supply of water, they would build their homes nearby. They would plant

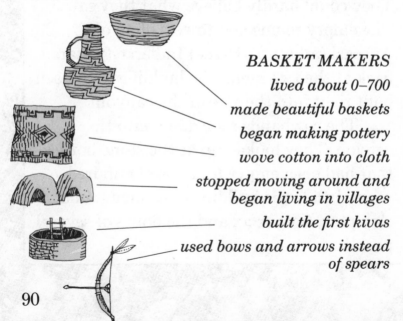

BASKET MAKERS
lived about 0–700
made beautiful baskets
began making pottery
wove cotton into cloth
stopped moving around and
began living in villages
built the first kivas
used bows and arrows instead
of spears

their thirsty crops—cotton, corn, beans, squash and tobacco. The soil would be fed by the stream, lake or water hole.

In the beginning, the Anasazi were called the Basket Makers. They lived out in the open at first, often traveling from place to place. These people were known as the Basket Makers because they made beautiful baskets. They do not seem to have had clay pots, bowls and other pieces of pottery.

Around the year 500, changes began to happen in the Basket Makers' way of life. They no longer moved around. Instead, they lived in villages. More and more, they farmed rather than hunted for food.

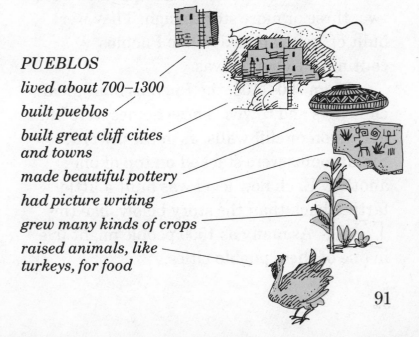

PUEBLOS
lived about 700–1300
built pueblos
built great cliff cities and towns
made beautiful pottery
had picture writing
grew many kinds of crops
raised animals, like turkeys, for food

91

These Basket-Maker Anasazi also made pottery for the first time. This skill of pottery making was probably learned from other Indians that lived to the south.

The Basket Makers started building large round structures partly or completely below the ground. These structures were called *kivas* (KEE-vahz). Kivas were not houses. They were places in which special meetings were held.

By the year 700, the Anasazi were no longer called Basket Makers. They were known as the Pueblos because they put up buildings called *pueblos*. Their pueblos were two, three or more stories high. They were built of stone and clay. The Pueblos continued to build kivas.

From 900–1100, the Pueblos built great cliff cities and towns. These homes were built in canyon or cliff walls, as in Mesa Verde. Small rooms were stacked on top of one another. Each new level was built a little farther back than the story below, like this: As many as 1500 people might live in one of these pueblo cities.

A Kiva at Mesa Verde

The cliff pueblos were especially good for protection. There were few doors on the ground floor. The people used ladders to reach the first roof. If an enemy group of Indians attacked, the Pueblos just pulled up the ladders and fought from the housetops. The Pueblos also reached their homes by cutting hidden paths and steps into the rock.

By 1100, the Anasazi were a great people. They did beautiful pottery work. They had picture writing. They knew how to grow many kinds of crops. They even raised turkeys for food. Life was good.

But by 1300, the Pueblos were gone from their cliff homes. No one knows what really happened. Today most people believe the Pueblo way of life changed for two reasons. First, there was scarcely any rain in the area for over 20 years. And second, other Indians began moving onto the land. These new Indians were hunters and fighters. They attacked the Pueblos' cities and towns.

The Pueblos probably couldn't withstand both the attacks and the lack of life-giving rain. Most likely, they left their cliff homes and moved out onto the flat land. There they mixed with other Indian peoples. So over the last few hundred years, the people called the Anasazi disappeared. But their magnificent cities remain.

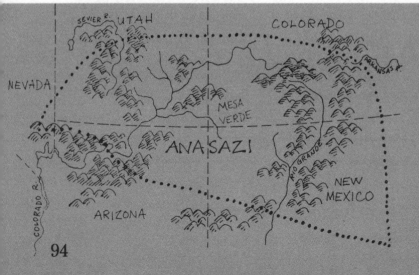

SPECIAL WORDS *vocabulary*

Match each word with its meaning. Write the letters in the blanks.

Words
1. Anasazi ___
2. pottery ___
3. kivas ___

Meanings
a. round, underground structures
b. the Ancient Ones
c. things made of clay

🔑 52 • *Best Score 3* • *My Score* ___

WHAT DID THEY DO? *classification/outline*

Write 1 next to the thing the Basket Makers (0–700) did and 2 next to what the Pueblos (700–1300) did.

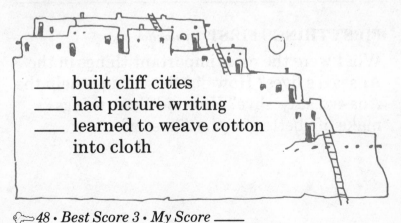

___ built cliff cities
___ had picture writing
___ learned to weave cotton
into cloth

🔑 48 • *Best Score 3* • *My Score* ___

THE ANASAZI PEOPLE   *inferences*

Check (✔) the four things listed below that would probably have been true of the Anasazi.

____ 1. peaceful
____ 2. built large boats and sailed them
____ 3. hunted with guns
____ 4. lived in many parts of the United States
____ 5. smart
____ 6. loved beautiful things and made beautiful pottery
____ 7. learned how to make pottery from other Indians
____ 8. met Christopher Columbus

☞125 • Best Score 4 • My Score ____
All Best Scores 10 • All My Scores ____

___

FIRST THINGS FIRST   *evaluation*

What were the most important things in the Anasazi's lives? How did these things help the Anasazi stay alive? How did these things make life better for the Anasazi?